THE UNITED STATES GOVERNMENT

HOUSE OF REPRESENTATIVES

FRANCIE DOLAN

NorwoodHouse Press

Cataloging-in-Publication Data

Names: Dolan, Francie.
Title: House of Representatives / Francie Dolan.
Description: Buffalo, NY : Norwood House Press, 2027. | Series: The United States government | Includes glossary and index.
Identifiers: ISBN 9781978581494 (pbk.) | ISBN 9781978581500 (library bound) | ISBN 9781978581517 (ebook)
Subjects: LCSH: United States. Congress. House--Juvenile literature.
Classification: LCC JK1319.D65 2027 | DDC 328.73072--dc23

Published in 2027 by
Norwood House Press
2544 Clinton Street
Buffalo, NY 14224

Designer: Rhea Magaro
Editor: Tricia Hoffman

Photo credits: Cover, p. 1 Rob Crandall/Shutterstock.com; Cover, p. 1 Sergey Kamshylin/Shutterstock.com; p. 5 VectorMine/Shutterstock.com; pp. 6, 8 Wikipedia; p. 7 National Gallery of Art; p. 9 Library of Congress; pp. 10, 17 The White House; p. 11 U.S. Census/Shutterstock.com; p. 12 Gary Blakeley/Shutterstock.com; p. 13 DCStockPhotography/Shutterstock.com; p. 14 DHS photo by Tara Molle/Shutterstock.com; p. 15 Joyce N. Boghosian/Shutterstock.com; p. 16 polartgraphics/Shutterstock.com; p. 18 Michael MLPG/Shutterstock.com; p. 19 Christopher Penler/Shutterstock.com; p. 21 Philip Yabut/Shutterstock.com;

Printed in the United States of America

TABLE OF CONTENTS

THE UNITED STATES GOVERNMENT

The United States **Constitution** tells how the nation's government is organized. There are three parts, or branches. They are the executive branch, **legislative** branch, and judicial branch.

The House of Representatives is part of the legislative branch.

BRANCHES OF GOVERNMENT

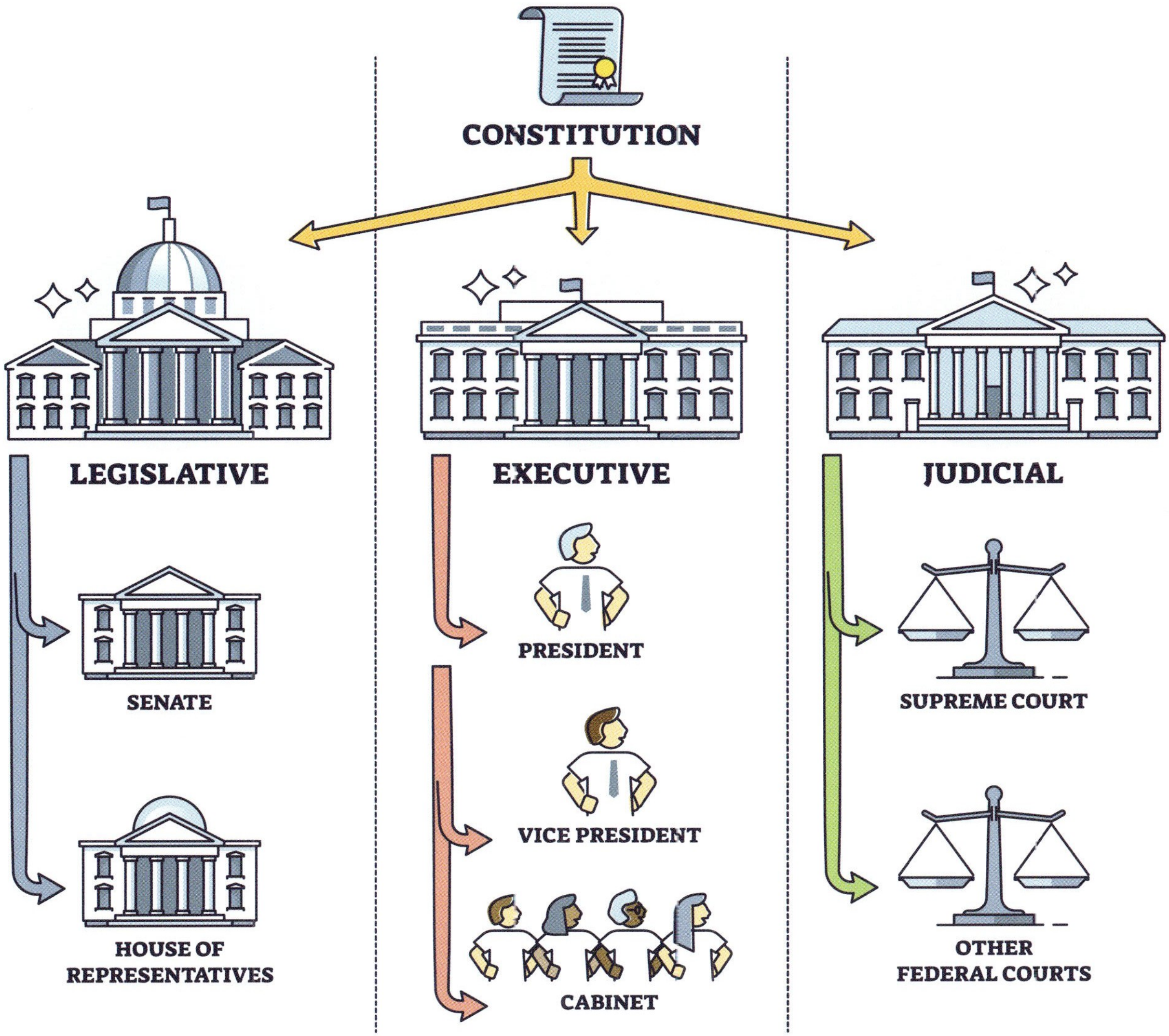

THE PEOPLE'S HOUSE

The writers of the U.S. Constitution had to decide how people would be represented by legislators in **Congress** to vote on laws for the country.

States with many people wanted representation to be based on population. Small states did not want to be ignored.

The Great **Compromise** settled the issue. Congress would have two parts, or houses. The Senate would be based on states. Each state would get two senators.

The House of Representatives would be based on population. More populous states would get more representatives than states with fewer people.

The House of Representatives is also called the House or the "People's House." It has 435 members, or representatives.

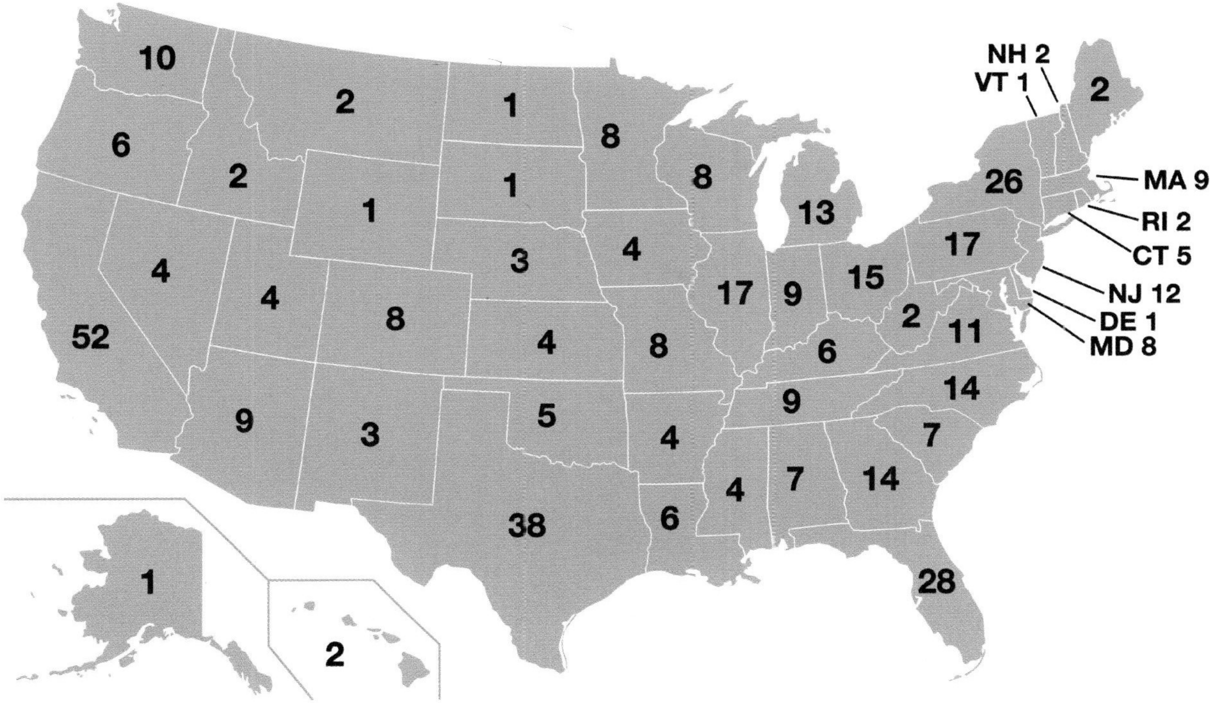

The country is divided into 435 districts. People in each district vote for a representative. Texas has 38 districts. Alaska has one district. Each district has about 750,000 people. As populations change, districts change too.

The House meets in one wing of the U.S. Capitol Building in Washington, D.C. When an American flag flies over that side of the building, the House is in session.

Representatives are elected for two-year **terms**. There is no limit on how many terms they can serve. They must be at least 25 years old. They must be U.S. citizens. They must live in the state they represent.

POWERS AND RESPONSIBILITIES

Representatives work in **committees** to understand the needs of the country. They write **bills** to suggest new laws.

House leaders, including the Speaker of the House, decide which bills go to the House floor for **debate** and voting.

If a bill passes the House, it goes to the Senate for a vote. Before a bill can become law, both houses must pass it.

The U.S. president signs the approved bill. Then, it is a new law. If the president will not sign, and two-thirds of Congress still votes yes, the bill becomes law.

Tax laws must begin as bills in the House. This means that decisions about people's money get made by the part of government closest to the people.

Along with the Senate, the House has the power to declare war. It can **impeach** the president.

GOVERNING THE UNITED STATES

Representatives have important jobs. They represent their **constituents**. They make laws.

What district do you live in? Who represents it? How do his or her decisions affect you?

SAVES LIVES!
USAID
CLOSED
COMING SOON
CHINA'S HEGEMONY
THE FACES

GLOSSARY

bills (bilz): written plans for new laws to be debated and voted on by legislators

committees (kuh-MIT-eez): groups of people chosen to discuss issues and make decisions for a larger group; House committees include the Budget Committee and the Natural Resources Committee

compromise (KAHM-pruh-mize): an agreement that accepts something that is not entirely what you wanted in order to satisfy some of the requests of other people

Congress (KAHNG-gris): the part of the U.S. government that makes laws and that includes the House of Representatives and the Senate; the legislative body of the United States

constituents (kuhn-STICH-oo-uhnts): voters represented by an elected official; people who live in a congressional district represented by a member of the House

constitution (kahn-sti-TOO-shuhn): a document that sets forth the basic laws of a country and that outlines the rights of its people and the power of its government

debate (di-BATE): discussion in which people express different opinions and ideas

impeach (im-PEECH): to remove an official from their position for breaking a rule or committing a crime

legislative (lej-is-LAY-tive): related to the branch of government that makes and changes laws for the country

terms (turmz): definite or set periods of time; members of the House of Representatives are elected to terms that last two years

THINKING QUESTIONS

1. Which branch of the U.S. government includes the House of Representatives?
2. What was the Great Compromise?
3. How many representatives are in the House? Why?
4. How does a bill become a law?
5. Why do tax bills begin in the House?

INDEX

ABOUT THE AUTHOR

Francie Dolan is a writer from Seattle, Washington. She is an American history buff who loves to learn about how her country works and how it has changed over time. She jumps at the chance to travel to Washington, D.C., and visit the capital's important buildings and monuments.